SEW CUTE!

T0317824

Tiny
FELT
CUTIES
& Creatures

DELILAH IRIS

Walter Foster

© 2023 Quarto Publishing Group USA Inc.
Text and photos © 2023 Delilah Iris

First published in 2023 by Walter Foster Publishing, an imprint of The Quarto Group. 100 Cummings Center, Suite 265D, Beverly, MA 01915, USA.
T (978) 282-9590 **F** (978) 283-2742 **www.quarto.com** • **www.walterfoster.com**

Walter Foster Publishing titles are also available at discount for retail, wholesale, promotional, and bulk purchase. For details, contact the Special Sales Manager by email at specialsales@quarto.com or by mail at The Quarto Group, Attn: Special Sales Manager, 100 Cummings Center, Suite 265D, Beverly, MA 01915, USA.

ISBN: 978-0-7603-8052-9

Digital edition published in 2023
eISBN: 978-0-7603-8053-6

Design & Page Layout: Cindy Samargia Laun

Printed in China
10 9 8 7 6 5 4 3 2 1

SEW CUTE!

Tiny
FELT
CUTIES
& Creatures

DELILAH IRIS

Walter Foster

TABLE OF CONTENTS

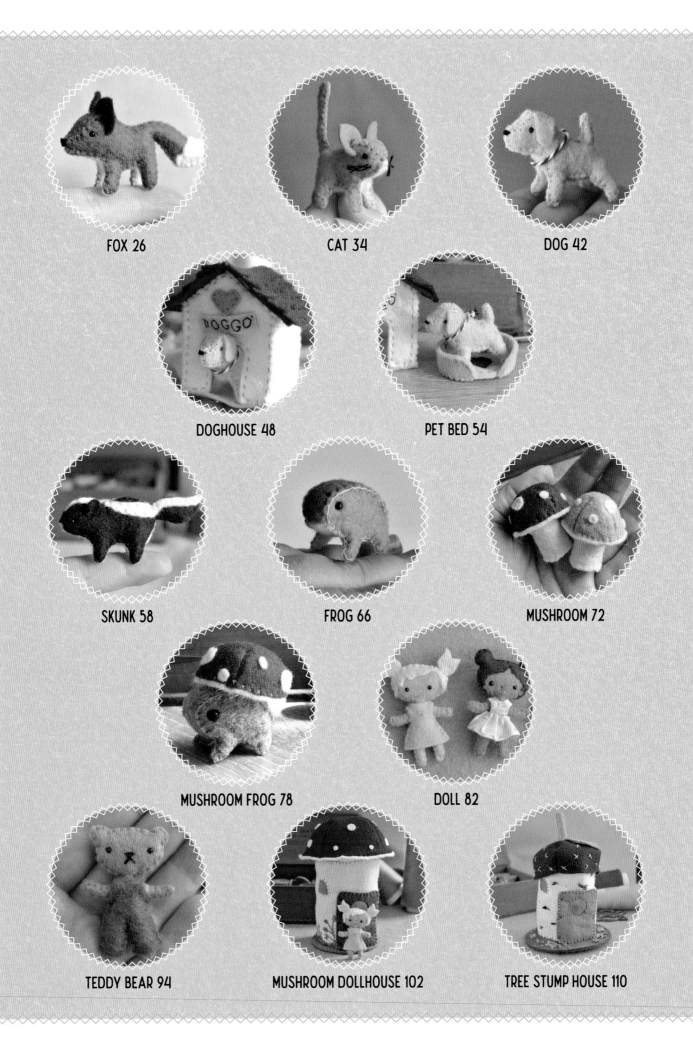

INTRODUCTION

Welcome to *Tiny Felt Cuties & Creatures*, where you'll find just about the cutest miniature felt animal and doll sewing projects in existence!

This book has been a long, long time in the making. I've been fascinated with tiny things, miniatures, and tiny fairy worlds since I was a child. I often created tiny forts when I was a child and filled them with miniatures and trinkets, even a tiny tea set. I imagined what it would feel like to be a tiny forest creature and live in a mushroom house or a tree stump. This love has lived on in me and in my work throughout my entire life!

In writing this book, I have combined my love of tiny things with a very real desire to find a use for all of the felt scraps I've had lying around from other projects. The projects in this book are absolutely perfect for using up even the tiniest of felt scraps. These projects don't require many tools or extraordinary skills to create. Because they are so small, you can bring your crafts with you on the go, and they won't take up very much of your time either.

The best part is that with my step-by-step instruction and detailed pictures, you can create the most charming and sweet tiny creatures that will surely delight your friends and family. These little critters make the most fabulous gifts or miniature pets to pop in your pocket. Create entire sets with my miniature felt accessories and doll houses. These projects are designed to mix and match and interchange together!

Besides, special, tiny, handmade gifts are the best kind of gifts! There's nothing like handmade present to show that you really do care.

While creating the projects in this book, I have combined some of the crafts and skills that are nearest and dearest to my heart: wool felt and hand sewing! I love the simplicity and rustic feel of both. Felt has such an earthy and whimsical nature; crafts created from felt always hold just a bit more magic and whimsy for me. It's also very forgiving in nature for those who are new to crafting and stitching.

Hand sewing is one of the oldest traditional skills you can learn. I love how minimalistic this craft can be, requiring nothing more than a needle or two and some good all-purpose thread. With few tools and expenses, you can get started creating piles of tiny creatures and dolls while honing a skill that is useful in so many ways!

Let's get started creating just about the cutest tiny creatures you could ever dream of!

TOOLS & MATERIALS

One of the things I love most about making felt miniatures is that almost anyone can get started with this hobby without breaking the bank.

Because the projects are small, you can make them with your leftover scraps, and tiny craft projects are easy to take on the go. Bring your tiny crafts on vacation to work on during your downtime. Make miniatures in the waiting room of a doctor's office or craft with a friend!

Here are the tools and supplies that I use most often while making tiny felt creatures.

HAND-SEWING NEEDLES

This inexpensive sewing supply can be found in the craft section of big-box stores, as well as in your local craft- or sewing-supply store. I like to keep two types of hand-sewing needles in my supply stash at all times.

- **Size 10 hand-sewing sharps:** Size-10 sharps are very small and thin, which makes these needles perfect for tiny stitches close to the edges of your seams.
- **Size 5 embroidery needle:** Embroidery needles are slightly bigger to accommodate thicker threads, such as embroidery floss. The needle's eye is slightly larger. I often switch back and forth between a size 5 and 10 needle within any given project.

Other items you may want to consider:

- **Beading needles (optional):** I keep beading needles on hand for adding seed beads to any felt project. Seed beads make for fantastic doll eyes, in addition to adding a pop of bling to your project!
- **Needle threader (optional):** For anyone who gets frustrated trying to thread a needle, this nifty and affordable tool can be a life saver!

WHICH TYPES OF THREAD SHOULD I USE?

The threads used for the projects in this book are fairly inexpensive and easy to find. Here's what to keep in your stash.

- **All-purpose sewing thread:**
  I find that all-purpose thread is the perfect weight and width for tiny sewing. It's easy to thread, but lightweight enough to create small, dainty stitches.
- **Six-strand embroidery floss:**
  I like to use embroidery floss to create small details, such as facial features and whiskers, as well as decorative details like flowers.

SEWING SCISSORS

A couple of pairs of good, sharp sewing scissors are essential. Here are my three favorites that I keep in my sewing tool kit.

- **Fiskars® Softgrip:**
  These very small but sharp scissors are perfect for cutting out tiny felt pieces featuring small curves and details.
- **Curved embroidery scissors:**
  I like a small set of curved scissors for cutting rounded curves on felt pieces. The curve of the scissor makes it an easier, more precise task.
- **Small standard embroidery scissors:**
  A very small set of embroidery scissors can be used for making cuts to tiny stitches, as well as close to threads.

TOY STUFFING

My go-to for stuffing felt miniatures, or really any stuffed toy, is Poly-fil®. The trick to stuffing miniatures with Poly-fil is to use very small bits of stuffing at a time. Ball up the stuffing into soft little beads by rolling it around between your fingers.

Why not buy beaded stuffing, you may ask? By beading the stuffing yourself, you can adjust the sizing of each ball of stuffing you fill into the miniature creature. Detailed parts such as limbs require very small beads of stuffing, whereas the body of a miniature felt creature can be filled with much bigger pieces of stuffing.

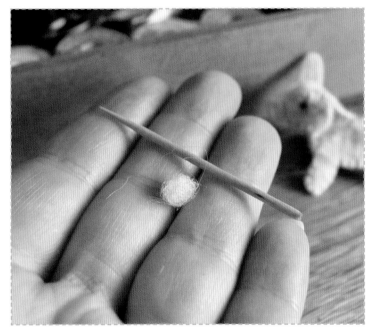

DIY STUFFING TOOLS

It's not always an easy task filling pieces of toy stuffing into your tiny felt creatures. At times it may seem downright impossible! But with the right set of tools, you can stuff your miniature felties with ease.

I like to use common, easily acquired items. One of my favorite tools is a toothpick. If you can get your hands on cocktail toothpicks, those are ideal. Cocktail toothpicks have one blunt end that's perfect for pushing small pieces of stuffing down into narrow spaces, such as limbs. But if you can't find cocktail toothpicks, regular ones are just fine. I like to snip one end of the toothpick off, removing the sharp point for a small, blunt-ended tool.

My second favorite tool is a large paper clip with one end bent open to create a metal stick with a handle on the end. Use the extended end of the paper clip to push the stuffing into your miniature creatures.

The last item in my DIY tool kit is a lollipop stick. These are best used for pushing stuffing into larger parts of tiny felt creatures, such as bodies and heads. The end of the stick is wider, making it easier to push larger pieces into place.

DOLL EYES

Each miniature creature needs a pair of eyes, and there are many ways to create this feature. My favorite but most difficult to find are plastic safety eyes. For tiny felt creatures, you will need 1 to 3 mm doll eyes, which are not usually readily available in craft stores but make for the cutest felt miniatures. Safety eyes come with a post protruding from the back of the eye. The post of the eye is installed onto the felt by creating a small hole and fitting a small washer over the post, which holds the eye in place on the felt.

The next best alternative to traditional doll eyes, seed beads are available in a variety of colors and are easily found in most craft and sewing stores. Seed beads must be sewn into place. I find it looks best when I try to match the color of the thread to the color of the safety eye when sewing it into place.

The third and most inexpensive method for creating eyes on felt creatures is sewing in the eyes with embroidery thread. A simple cluster of small stitches placed side by side will suffice to create a small circular shape. I recommend splitting your embroidery thread to two to three strands to create details on miniature creations.

TAPE

I always have a roll or two of wide, clear packing tape on hand for cutting felt pieces from a pattern. My favorite is Duck® brand, but any clear, wide tape will do.

Roughly cut the pattern piece from paper, leaving some space between the pattern edges and your cut. Lay the pattern onto your chosen felt, and then lay a piece of wide tape over the pattern, affixing it to the felt. Next, simply cut on the lines of the pattern with some small, sharp precision shears, cutting through the tape, pattern paper, and felt all at the same time. The tape holds the pattern in place on the felt, allowing for very precise and clean cuts.

CUSTOMIZE YOUR CREATURES WITH ART SUPPLIES!

I always keep some art supplies on hand, such as chalk pastels and watercolor and gouache paints. I use these for adding customization and a few more fine details that might not translate well with embroidery. Some examples include using chalk pastel in a rosy color to add blushing cheeks to a tiny doll.

Another idea is to paint spots and color variations onto animals. Paint the spots on a dog or mittens on a cat! You can also use fine-tipped markers or paint pens to add stripes to cats.

2

Basics of

HAND
SEWING

Hand stitching is one of the most useful and rewarding skills you can learn. This skill has been practiced for centuries, and it has many, many uses, both creative and practical.

I have been sewing since I was a child. I grew up among women who honed this craft using both hand stitching and machine sewing. It has always been second nature for me to want to make something with my hands using fabric scraps and bits of sewing notions. As a child, I would tear up old T-shirts to make teddy bears and sew circle skirts from old bedsheets.

I will share with you the hand sewing and embroidery stitches that I like to use most in my felt creations. My hope is that you will find these stitches helpful in everyday life, in creative projects, or just to sew back on that old button that keeps falling off.

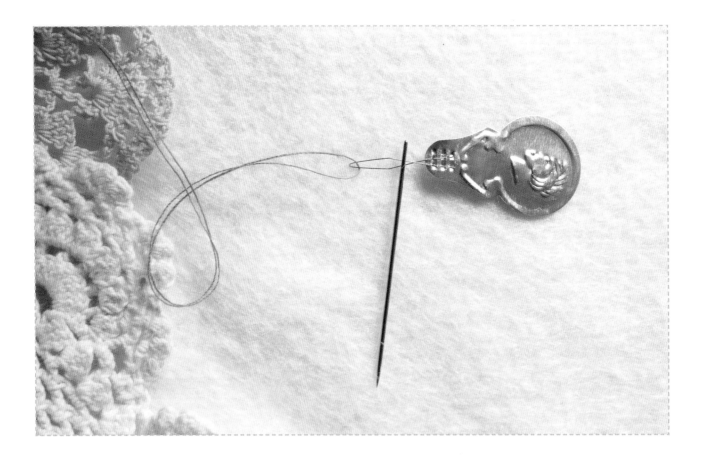

THE BASICS: THREADING A NEEDLE & KNOTTING YOUR THREAD

Every hand-sewing project begins with threading a needle. I'm a simple gal, so I almost always use the good ol' method of wetting the end of the thread and threading the needle by eye. However, there are a couple tricks for those of you frustrated by this method.

For one, there is the needle threader. It's inexpensive and easily found in stores. To use it, you simply insert the end of the threader through the eye of the needle. Insert the thread into the end of the tool, and simply pull through the eye of the needle, bringing the thread through.

If you don't have a needle threader on hand, another method is to vigorously rub the eye of the needle over the thread until it pops through.

Once the thread is through the needle, the next step is to double up the thread by pulling the end all the way through so that both ends of the thread are together. Knot the thread together at the end.

One way to knot the thread is to wrap the thread around the needle several times, overlapping threads while you're wrapping. Pull the needle through the layers of wrapped thread, and pull the thread through until a knot forms at the end of the length of thread.

A simpler method is to simply make a doubled-up knot at the end of the thread.

STARTING YOUR STITCHING

STEP 1

I start my stitching by inserting the needle through one felt pattern piece, placing the knot on the inside of the project. Always try to hide your beginning and end stitches! The knot will be hidden between the two pieces of felt for a seamless start and end to your stitching.

STEP 2

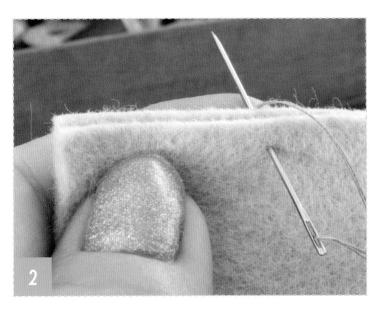

The next step is to make your first stitch into a knot. Send the needle through the felt layers on the opposite side of the project, creating one stitch loop through two layers of felt.

STEP 3

Send the needle through the loop and pull tight. You've just secured your stitching with a knot holding the layers in place. Time to begin stitching!

Basics of Hand Sewing

HAND STITCHES

Blanket Stitch

My absolute favorite stitch to use in hand-sewing projects, the blanket stitch is incredibly durable and creates a nice, clean edge. The blanket stitch is a popular stitch often seen around the edges of fleece blankets, designed to hold the edges from curling or fraying. Think of the blanket stitch as making your first knotted stitch in a project—creating this stitch over and over all along the seam edges of your project.

Begin by knotting the thread and sending it through the felt near the edge, as described in "Starting Your Stitching" (page 17). Once your felt pattern pieces have been layered together and you've made your first knotted stitch, you are then ready to blanket stitch. Send the needle through the felt just next to your first stitch. Pull the thread through the back until you have just a small loop above the raw edge. Insert the needle through the loop and pull tight to hold the layers but not so tight that the fabric buckles. Continue stitching this way all along the edge to create a blanket stitch.

Whipstitch

The whipstitch is very easy to learn and great for quickly stitching projects.

Sewing a whipstitch is simple. Start by knotting the thread and sending it through the felt near the seam edge as demonstrated on page 17. Creating this stitch is done just as it sounds! Insert the needle through the layers of felt, and then "whip" the needle around to the front of the project again for your next stitch. Repeat. It's as simple as that!

Running Stitch

Running stitch is the most basic stitch of all. It just means stitching in a dashed line formation. I like to use this to topstitch layers of felt together.

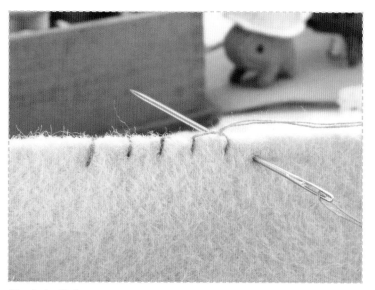

Blanket stitch

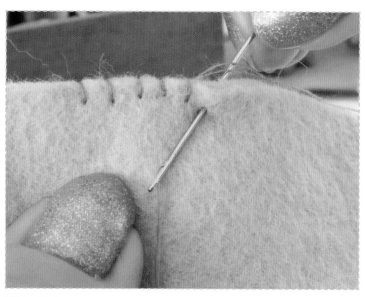

Whipstitch

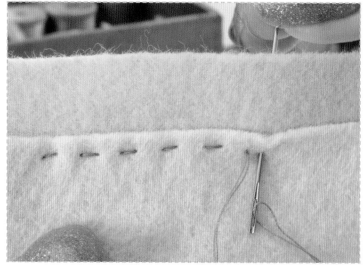

Running stitch

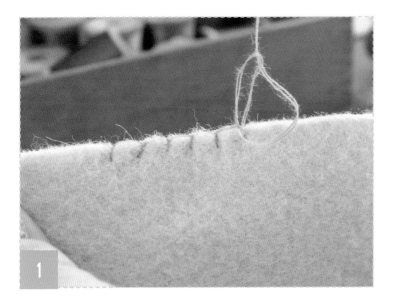

ENDING & TYING OFF STITCHES

Just like when I'm starting a stitch, I prefer to hide my knots and loose ends when ending my stitching. It's incredibly easy to do with felt because it's such a forgiving material to work with. There are two ways that I like to hide my end stitches and loose ends of thread. One method is to hide it among the stitching. The other is to send the thread out of the opposite side of the work, leaving a long tail end on the inside of the piece.

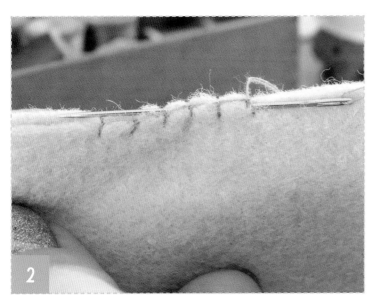

STEP 1

Begin by making a knot at the end of your work, same as with your beginning stitch.

STEP 2

Next, insert your needle into the felt along the row of stitching.

STEP 3

Pull the needle out along the row of stitching, about ½ to 1 inch (1⅓ to 2½ cm) from your ending knot. Pull the thread tight and snip close to the edge. Be very careful not to accidentally cut your stitches.

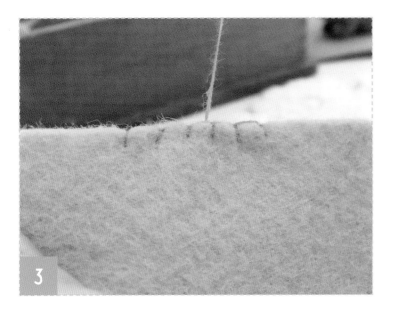

If you're wary of accidentally cutting your stitching, you can go a step further and insert the needle back into the stitching and out the bottom or back of the piece you are sewing. Pull it tightly and snip as close to the felt as possible.

If the end of the thread shows, simply rub the felt a bit and it will get pushed back inside your creation.

BASTING STITCH

The basting stitch is used to create gathers for a ruffled appearance. A very easy stitch to achieve, the basting stitch is essentially a loose running stitch with the ends left rather loose so you can pull the threads to create a gather. The most important element of creating this stitch is trying to keep the stitches uniform for a consistent ruffled appearance, where each pleat is approximately the same size. The basting stitch is designed to be snipped and pulled out after you've completed your project.

To create a basting stitch, begin by knotting your thread to one end. Create a long and loose running stitch (page 18) along the top of your fabric or felt.

Create the stitch across the top edge of your piece, running from one end to the other. Leave your threads dangling, and then hold the thread while you push the fabric along the stitch to create the gathered ruffle.

Usually, you will then iron the top of the ruffle and stitch it into place with a running or whip stitch. Once the ruffle holds in place correctly, you can snip the basting stitch and pull it out. I usually use this stitch with cotton fabric for doll clothes, but it can also be used in certain felt projects, such as flowers or the underside of a mushroom.

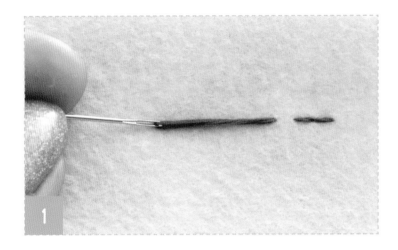

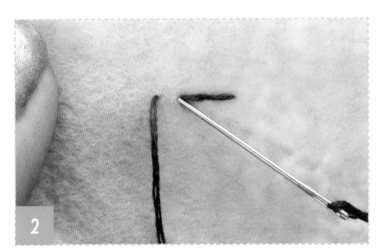

EMBROIDERY STITCHES

Embroidery stitches can be used to add decorative detail to your felt creations—either through pretty, embroidered flowers and decoration, or simply to add eyes and facial features.

Backstitch
This is one of my favorite embroidery stitches. I use backstitch in line work, to create flower stems, and more. To create a backstitch, begin by making a single small stitch as with a running stitch (page 18). Insert the threaded needle as if you are about to create the next stitch in a running stitch. However, instead of stitching forward, move backward, inserting the needle at the end of the first stitch.

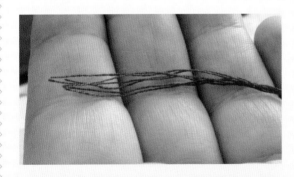

⟩⟩⟩ SPLITTING THREAD ⟨⟨⟨

One important step when creating tiny embroidery for miniatures is splitting your embroidery thread. This will make it smaller and facilitate more delicate detail. Standard embroidery thread comes with six strands twisted together. Each project in this book may call for splitting into different sizes, such as two or three strands.

To split the thread, all you need to do is twist the end of the embroidery thread in your fingers until it unravels just a bit.

Split one side of the thread into however many strands you need for the project, and then gently pull apart. After splitting the thread, you may want to gently roll the thread in your fingers again to wind it back together.

Basics of Hand Sewing

French Knot

I love to use a French knot to add decorative details to a project. French knots can be used to make rosebuds, moss, and even doll eyes.

Knot your thread and insert it into the felt, leaving the knot at the back. Wrap the thread around the needle three times, keeping the needle close to the top of the project.

Insert the needle into the felt again, very close to the first stitch, making sure to keep the thread wrapped on the needle and holding the loose end of thread down with your thumb.

Continuing to hold the end of thread under your thumb, pull the needle through the felt until it holds the wrapped "knot" in place.

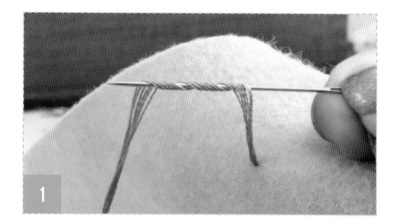

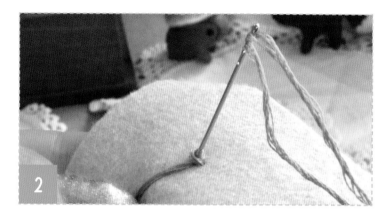

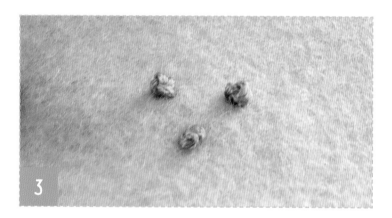

You'll use the French knot to create these cute flowers in the tree stump house project on pages 110-117!

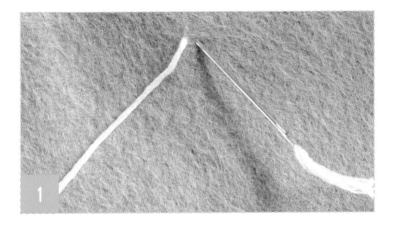

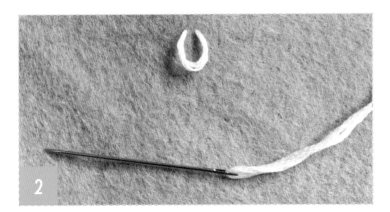

Lazy Daisy Stitch

The lazy daisy is another great stitch that can be used to create a variety of decorative details. My favorite way to use this stitch is to create flower petals or even leaves.

Begin by knotting the thread and inserting it into the felt, leaving the knot at the back or inside of the project. Insert the needle into the felt again, just next to the first thread.

Pull the thread through the felt until you have a small loop at the top of the felt.

Insert the needle from the back, bringing the thread through at the inside end of the loop. Next, insert it on the opposite side of the end of the loop, holding the thread in place on the surface of the felt.

Repeating this stitch in a formation will create a small daisy flower!

Basics of Hand Sewing

3

TEENY-TINY CRITTERS

& Their Accessories

FOX

Miniature felt foxes make beautiful pocket-sized companions. These beauties have been near and dear to my heart since childhood, when I used to spot them during my adventures roaming the forest behind my home. And even more recently, my children and I watch the foxes that live in the fields. Foxes are among my favorites of all the wild woodland creatures.

Pattern on page 119

STEP 1

Begin by cutting the fox pattern from felt scraps. For the best results, I recommend a copper- or rust-colored felt to create the standard red fox, or a deep gray-and-black combination for a gray fox. I always use white felt for the tip of the tail and the underside of the body, as well as dark brown or black for the ears.

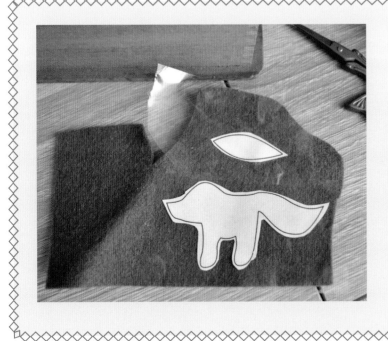

››› CUTTING TIPS ‹‹‹

The best way to cut miniature felt pieces with precision is by taping the pattern pieces directly to the felt. To do this, begin by roughly trimming the pattern piece from the paper it's printed on. Use wide, clear packing tape to hold the pattern onto your chosen felt.

Trim the pattern from the felt directly on the pattern lines with small, sharp scissors.

STEP 2

Next, add a set of eyes to the fox using doll eyes or embroidery felt, or by sewing on black seed beads.

When using safety eyes (plastic bulbs that can be used for eyes), I like to use a 1- to 3-mm tiny black safety eye. To install the eyes, pair both of the fox body pieces together. This ensures that both eyes will be installed in the same spot on both sides of the fox's face.

Use a pin to find the placement of the eye. Use a toothpick or the end of your scissors to carefully make a small hole for installing the post of the doll eye. Send the end of the eye post into the hole at each side of the face. Push the small washer over the back of the eye post to hold it in place. Snip off the excess end of the eye post with scissors.

Embroidery thread is another option for adding eyes to your miniature fox. Begin by pairing the fox body pieces and using a pin to find the best eye placement.

With a black marker, create a small dot on either side of the face using the hole marked with the pin as a guide.

Cut a piece of six-strand black embroidery thread about 5 inches long and split it down to three strands. Thread your needle with a piece of the split embroidery thread and knot it at the end. Make tiny stitches on the fox's face using the black dots as a guide, covering the dots to make a circular shape.

STEP 3

Next, add the white fur piece to the end of the tail. Sewing just across the top of the tail piece, stitch the tip of the tail into place using white thread and a basic running stitch.

STEP 4

Thread a needle and knot the thread at the end. Match and pin the underside of the body to one side of the fox's body piece and pin at the legs. Begin stitching at the back of the fox just at the inside base of the tail.

Teeny-Tiny Critters & Their Accessories

STEP 5

Sew together at the edges of the felt using a short, tight blanket or whipstitch. Sew along the edge moving past both legs, up the chest, and ending at the front of the face.

STEP 6

Pin the opposite side of the fox's body into place. Begin stitching again, but this time, start at the top of the fox just before the tail. Sew the edges together, moving toward the tip of the tail. Switch thread colors when you reach the white felt at the top of the tail. Switch once again, using a rust or gray thread at the underside of the tail.

STEP 7

When you reach the front of the fox's face, match the front face piece to one side of the body and sew it into place from front to back.

STEP 8

Next, begin stuffing the fox with polyester toy stuffing. The best way to stuff tiny creatures is by balling up the stuffing in very small pieces at a time. Begin by stuffing the legs, balling up small pieces of Poly-Fil and pushing them into the legs with a toothpick. Continue stuffing the fox this way, filling all four legs and the tail.

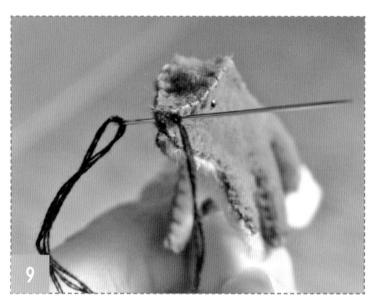

STEP 9

Return to sewing the fox by threading a needle and knotting the end, and begin sewing the opposite side of the fox's face into place. When you've reached about the top of the head, leave the thread dangling for a moment while you add a tiny, embroidered nose.

Thread a second needle with black embroidery thread, split down to two or three strands. Knot the end of the thread. Send the needle into the inside of the fox's head through the unsewn opening and out one side of the face just where the nose would sit.

STEP 10

Pull the needle through and insert it again at the opposite side of the face. Pull the needle through to the opposite side to create a tiny stitch at the tip of the face.

Repeat once or twice to create a tiny black nose. Send the needle back into the inside of the body and out of the unsewn opening. Trim the end and tuck any excess into the body.

Teeny-Tiny Critters & Their Accessories

STEP 11

Continue sewing where you left off at the top of the head, sewing until there is just a small opening left big enough to finish stuffing the fox. Stuff the head and body until full. Sew the last opening shut, knot your thread, and trim the excess.

STEP 12

Next, position the ears and pin them into place. Thread a needle and knot the end to begin stitching the ears using a very small whipstitch at the base of the ears.

Once both ears are sewn in place,
your miniature fox is finished!

Teeny-Tiny Critters & Their Accessories

CAT

House cats come in an array of colors and patterns, so these little
kitties are so much fun to get creative with! Make them in just
about any color, and add stripes or spots with different colors
of felt, wool, embroidery, and even paint.

STEP 1

Begin by cutting the cat pattern from any color of felt using the methods on page 27.

Add a set of eyes to the cat using doll eyes, embroidery felt, or seed beads. See page 12 for more on creating eyes for your miniature toys.

Pattern on page 119

STEP 2

Next, let's add an extra-special detail to the cat and give your little cutie character. Let's add some whiskers!

Use 6-strand black embroidery thread to make the whiskers. Start by splitting a 3- to 4-inch (7½ to 10 cm) piece of embroidery thread down to 3 strands, leaving you with 2 pieces of 3-strand embroidery thread. Place a knot about 1 inch (2½ cm) or so in from one end on each piece.

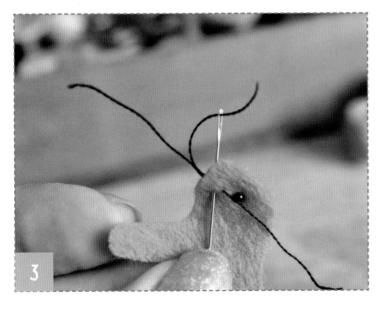

STEP 3

Send the needle through the felt where you want to place the first whisker. When the needle is about three-quarters of the way through the felt, thread the end with one strand of thread from the knotted end of the embroidery thread.

Teeny-Tiny Critters & Their Accessories

STEP 4

Pull the threaded needle through the felt to bring the whisker to the front of the face. Repeat this step twice more in slightly different places on the face to create the whiskers.

Repeat these steps on both pieces of felt so the cat will have whiskers on both sides of its face. The whiskers will be a tad too long at first; go back and trim both sides down a bit.

OPTIONAL

Add a tiny pink X to the underside piece of felt at the cat's bottom for a cheeky little detail.

STEP 5

Match the underside piece to one side of the cat and pin at the legs. Thread a needle and knot it at the end to begin stitching at the very back of the cat, just at the base of the tail. Sew together at the edges of the felt using a short, tight blanket or whipstitch. Sew along the edge moving past both legs, up the chest, and ending at the front of the face.

STEP 6

Pin the opposite side of the cat's body into place. Begin stitching again, this time starting at the top of the cat just before the tail. Sew the edges together, moving toward the tip of the tail.

STEP 7

Sew all along the edges until you reach just past the tip of the tail. To create a tail, use a pipe cleaner! Trim the pipe cleaner to fit inside the tiny cat; then insert the wire in the length of the tail, tucking the end into the back of the body. Continue sewing down the tail toward the back of the cat.

STEP 8

Continue sewing along the cat's body past both legs and up into the chest once more.

Teeny-Tiny Critters & Their Accessories

STEP 9

When you reach the front of the face, match the front face piece to one side of the face, starting from the nose. Stitch this piece into place on one side, sewing the edges together from the nose to the end of the piece.

>>> TIP <<<
The best way to stuff tiny creatures is by balling up the stuffing using separate, very small pieces.

STEP 10

Next, stuff the cat with Poly-Fil. Begin stuffing the legs by inserting tiny balls of Poly-Fil and pushing them into the legs with a toothpick. Continue this way, filling all four legs.

STEP 11

Return to sewing the cat by threading a needle, knotting the end, and sewing the opposite side of the cat's face into place. When you've reached the top of the head, leave the thread dangling for a moment while you add another face detail: a tiny pink nose!

Thread a second needle with pink embroidery thread split into two or three strands. Knot the end of the thread. Send the needle into the inside of the cat's head through the unsewn opening and out one side of the face just where the nose would sit.

STEP 12

Pull the needle through and insert it again at the opposite side of the face. Pull the needle through to create a tiny stitch at the tip of the face.

STEP 13

Repeat step 12 once or twice to create a tiny pink nose. Send the needle back into the inside of the body and out of the unsewn opening. Trim the end and tuck any excess into the body.

Teeny-Tiny Critters & Their Accessories

STEP 14

Continue sewing where you left off at the top of the head, sewing until there is just a small opening big enough to finish stuffing the kitty. Stuff the head and body until full.

STEP 15

Sew the last opening shut, knot your thread, and trim the excess.

STEP 16

Next, position the ears and pin them into place. Thread a needle and knot the end to begin stitching the ears into place using a very small whipstitch at the base of the ears.

Once both ears are sewn in place,
your tiny cat is finished!

DOG

Dog lovers and miniature enthusiasts, have I got the project
for you! What dollhouse isn't begging for its very own pet dog?
Making miniature felt dogs is so much fun because you can make
them in tons of colors! Create a spotted dog or add
tiny string collars too!

STEP 1

Begin by cutting the tiny dog pattern pieces from wool felt scraps in the color of your choice.

Pattern on page 120

STEP 2

Thread your sewing needle with a colored thread that coordinates with the felt, and knot the thread at the end. Pair the underbody dog pattern piece to one side of the dog's body pattern piece.

STEP 3

Begin stitching the two pattern pieces into place, beginning at the back base of the dog's tail. Stitch from the bottom of the tail and down the back leg using a short, tight blanket stitch or whipstitch.

Continue stitching the pieces together, moving along the edges past both legs and stopping at the front of the chest. Tie off your thread to the inside of the dog's body.

Teeny-Tiny Critters & Their Accessories

STEP 4

Attach the second main body piece to the tiny dog, once again pinning at the legs. Thread your needle and begin stitching at the top of the dog's back just before the tail.

STEP 5

Continue stitching along the edges of the pattern pieces past the tail, down the back legs, and toward the front of the chest again.

STEP 6

Stitch until you reach the tip of the nose. Pair the front face piece to one side of the main body piece from the tip of the nose. Continue stitching to hold the face piece in place.

STEP 7

When you reach the dog's ear, fold the ear downward and continue stitching to hold the ear in this position. Sew until you reach the back of the dog's head. Tie your thread off to the inside of the dog's body.

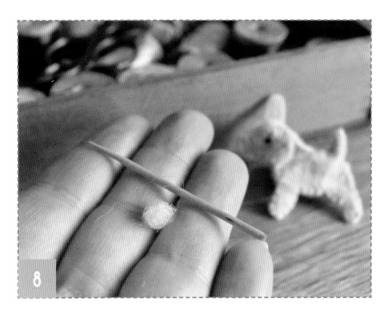

STEP 8

It's time to begin stuffing the tiny dog! Start by stuffing the legs with very small pieces of toy stuffing fiber. I like to ball up the pieces into small bead-sized pieces and push them into the legs with a toothpick. Stuff all four legs, and then the tail.

STEP 9

Thread your needle and return to sewing the front of the face at just the tip of the nose. Stitch together the opposite side of the face and ear. Stuff the head with small bits of toy stuffing. Sew to the back of the head, leaving a small opening and the thread and needle dangling for the meantime.

Teeny-Tiny Critters & Their Accessories

STEP 10

Now let's add a small, embroidered nose! Thread a needle with some black embroidery thread, knotted at the end. Send the needle through the opening at the back of the dog's head and out next to the tip of the nose.

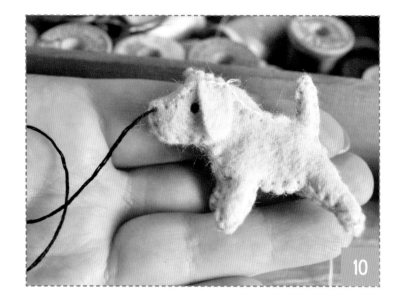

STEP 11

Send the needle back into the face on the opposite side, just next to the tip of the nose. Repeat once or twice, more placing small stitches on top of and directly next to each other until you like the look of the nose. Send the needle back into the head. Trim the excess thread and tuck the rest into the dog's body.

STEP 12

Continue stuffing the dog until it is completely full, and then sew the last bit of opening shut.

For a cute final detail, knot a small
piece of string or twine and tie it around the
dog's neck for a tiny collar. So cute!

Teeny-Tiny Critters & Their Accessories

Tiny Critter
Accessory!

DOGHOUSE

Every tiny dog needs a tiny doghouse! This cozy little pet abode
makes a perfect pairing with the tiny felt dog (pages 42-47), and it
is so fun to get creative with colors and decoration. Add colorful
details to your house and even your tiny pet's name!

STEP 1

Begin by cutting all the pattern pieces from the colored felt of your choice. I recommend cutting the walls from a different color than the roof and roof tiles. Choose a contrasting color to decorate the front of the house with a heart, fish, or bone. An earthy color should be used for the floors and name sign.

Pattern on page 121

STEP 2

Thread a needle and knot the end. Begin pairing double layers of all the outer walls of the doghouse and stitch them together with a running stitch. For this tutorial, I've used a contrasting- colored stitch, which adds a pretty, decorative touch.

STEP 3

When sewing the front of the house, you may want to sew the decorative details before doubling up the layers.

Teeny-Tiny Critters & Their Accessories

STEP 4

To sew the name sign, split a piece of six-strand embroidery thread into one or two strands. You can use a pencil or marker to write the name lightly before stitching it into the piece. Sew it to the front of the house by placing a single stitch at each side of the sign to resemble a nail.

STEP 5

Pair the front of the house with one of the side pieces and stitch together at the edges with a blanket or whipstitch.

STEP 6

Repeat this with the opposite side of the house, and then add the back of the house in place and stitch both sides.

STEP 7

Pair the two roof pieces and stitch them together at the top, again using a blanket or whip stitch.

STEP 8

Fit the roof to the top of the house and pin into place. Stitch them together with a whipstitch.

STEP 9

Pin the floor and stitch it into place with a whipstitch.

STEP 10

Lastly, add tiles to the top of the roof. These can be sewn into place; however, I recommend gluing them with a hot-glue gun or fabric glue. The tiles are meant to be staggered. To achieve this, flip every other tile in the opposite direction.

Once your tiny doghouse is finished,
it's ready for a tiny felt doggie
to be tucked safe inside!

PET BED

Cute hearts, fish, and bone pattern pieces add nice
decorative detailing to your pet beds and doghouses!

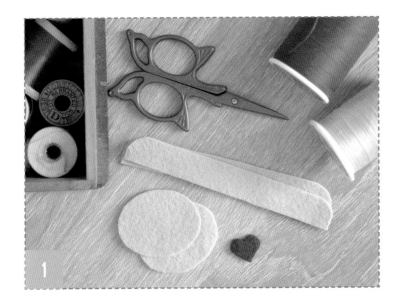

STEP 1

Begin by cutting the pet-bed pattern pieces from the colorful wool felt of your choice.

Pattern on page 120

STEP 2

To sew a decorative piece to the pet bed, begin by threading your needle with a contrasting color and knot at the end. Start sewing at the base piece of the pet bed. Stitch the piece into the middle of the base of the pet bed with a running stitch, tying your thread off at the back.

STEP 3

Pair two pieces of the pet bed base, and stitch them together at the edges with a running stitch.

Teeny-Tiny Critters & Their Accessories

STEP 4

Pair two pieces of the pet bed sides and stitch together with a running stitch. Stitch this piece along the curved top edge only.

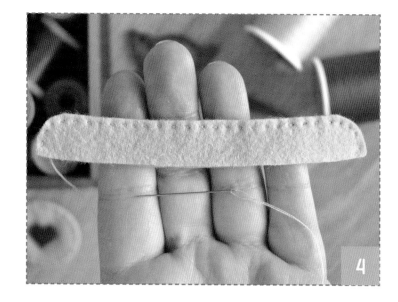

STEP 5

Find the middle of the side piece by folding it in half. Align the middle of this piece with the middle of the back base of the pet bed. Wrap the sides around the base, aligning at the bottom edges, and pin into place.

STEP 6

Stitch the sides to the bottom base using a blanket or a whipstitch.

Flip the bed over and it's done!

SKUNK

Skunks are at the top of my list of favorite woodland creatures.
While ridiculously cute, we often try to avoid them. But these little guys
are peaceful creatures, as well as beneficial since they feed on garden pests!
I learned this when a family of skunks moved in under my front porch and
I wanted to cohabitate with them rather than disturb the babies. The
more I learned about them, the more my fear turned into love for these
little cuties. I hope you enjoy creating this adorable miniature skunk.

STEP 1

Cut the skunk pattern from a combination of black and white felt scraps.

The main body pieces and top of the head should be cut from black felt. Cut the stripes, top of the head detail, and underside of the body from white felt.

Pattern on page 122

STEP 2

Match the skunk stripe pieces with the main skunk body pieces and sew into place with a small running stitch. Match the top of head detail piece to the top of the head piece and sew this into place as well.

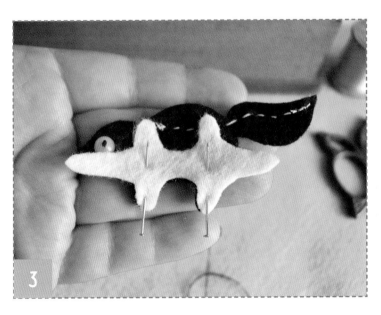

STEP 3

Match the white underside of the body piece with one of the main body pieces in black felt, and pin at the legs.

Teeny-Tiny Critters & Their Accessories

STEP 4

Thread a needle with black thread and knot one end of the thread. Begin sewing at the back of the skunk, just at the base of the tail, stitching together the edges of felt with a small, tight blanket or whipstitch.

STEP 5

Continue sewing along the edges of the felt past both legs and ending at the tip of the nose.

STEP 6

Match the top of the head piece in place and begin sewing from the tip of the nose. When you reach the end of the head piece, tie off the thread to the inside of the skunk's body.

Match the opposite side of the body in place, once again pinning at the legs. Make sure your needle is threaded with a long piece of black thread, and knot it at the end. Begin stitching at the top of the skunk's back, about ¼ inch (½ cm) from the top base of the tail.

STEP 7

Begin stitching the top edge of the skunk, moving toward the tip of the tail. Continue sewing all the way around the tail and past both legs on the opposite side of the skunk. When you reach the nose, begin sewing the opposite side of the face into place.

Teeny-Tiny Critters & Their Accessories

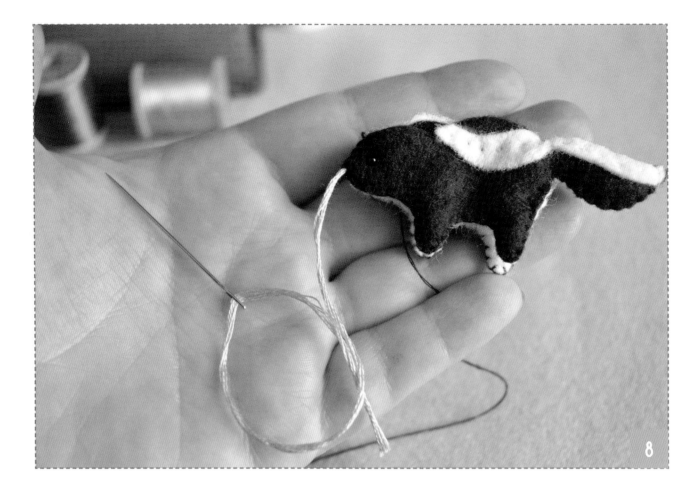

STEP 8

Stop sewing and let the thread dangle for a moment when you reach about three-quarters of the way down the side of the head.

Then add a cute little pink nose! Thread a needle with pink embroidery thread, knotted on the end. Send the needle through the opening at the back of the skunk's head and out just next to the tip of the nose.

STEP 9

Send the needle back into the face on the opposite side, just next to the tip of the nose.

STEP 10

Repeat this step once or twice more, placing small, pink stitches on top of and directly next to each other until you like the look of the nose.

STEP 11

Let's stuff the skunk! Begin by stuffing the legs with very small pieces of toy stuffing fiber. I like to ball up the pieces into small, bead-sized pieces and stuff them into the legs with a toothpick. Stuff all four legs to the tops, and then the tail.

STEP 12

Pick up the thread you left dangling earlier and continue sewing the skunk until there is just a small opening a little smaller than ½ inch (1 cm). Stuff the head and the rest of the body before stitching the last opening shut and tying off your thread.

Teeny-Tiny Critters & Their Accessories

STEP 13

Now it's time to add some tiny ears to the skunk! Begin by folding each ear at the base and making a stitch to hold the fold in place.

STEP 14

Snip the excess thread from the end of the stitch on one ear while leaving your thread dangling on the other. Pin the ears into place on the sides of the skunk's head.

STEP 15

Using the dangling thread that you left at one ear, stitch the ears into place with a whipstitch while also sending the needle straight through the skunk's head and out of the opposite ear.

Once the ears are sewn into place, tie off your thread at the back of one ear and snip off the excess thread. Your skunk is complete!

FROG

Frogs have held a magical place in my heart since I was a young girl spending rainy days splashing in puddles and roaming the woods in search of these small friends. Like tiny forest folk guarding toadstool mushroom rings and tree hollows, frogs are whimsical and endearing. No tiny woodland set would be complete without a frog or two!

STEP 1

Begin by cutting the frog pattern from felt. This frog can be made in all colors and combinations. After all, frogs in the wild come in all kinds of exotic colors! I like to cut the body and top of the frog in one color, with a contrasting color for the bottom of the frog.

Pattern on page 122

STEP 2

Add a set of eyes to the frog using doll eyes, embroidery felt, or seed beads. (See page 12 for more on creating eyes for your miniature toys.)

STEP 3

To begin sewing the frog, match the pattern pieces for the top and bottom of the frog at corresponding ends. Pin, place, and stitch together using either a blanket stitch or a whipstitch.

Teeny-Tiny Critters & Their Accessories

STEP 4

Thread your needle and create a knot at the end to begin stitching about three-quarters of the way down the frog's back.

STEP 5

Insert your needle so that the thread and needle dangle to the outside of the frog. Match one side of the frog body piece to the underside of the frog. Pin the pieces together at the legs.

STEP 6

Using a short, tight blanket or whipstitch, begin stitching the edges of the top of the frog together, moving toward the back of the frog and down the back leg.

STEP 7

Continue stitching along the legs, moving past both legs, up the chest, and past the face, ending where you first started your stitching. Send the needle to the inside of the frog. Knot the thread and trim the excess thread.

Teeny-Tiny Critters & Their Accessories

STEP 8

Flip the frog over and pin the opposite side into place to begin stitching in the same manner once again. This time, you're sewing the opposite side into place.

STEP 9

Sew along the outer edges in the same manner as on the first side, but this time, leave a space open for stuffing the frog.

Then, using very small amounts of polyester toy stuffing at a time, ball the stuffing up into pebble-sized pieces and stuff down into the legs with a toothpick. Fill all four legs, and then fill the rest of the body. Sew the last opening shut.

These cute little guys are so quick and
fun to stitch! Make them in two sizes:
tiny and teeny-tiny!

MUSHROOM

Tiny mushrooms make a perfect whimsical pairing for any woodland play set. These mushrooms are great accessories to our miniature woodland creatures and tiny dollhouses. They can even be used as hats for your little creatures!

STEP 1

Begin by cutting the mushroom pattern from colorful pieces of felt.

The mushroom caps can be made in a rainbow of colors, while the stems, base, and spots for the mushroom look best in a white or cream beige color.

Pattern on page 123

STEP 2

Pair the curved edges cut into the mushroom caps and stitch the edges together with a small, tight blanket or whipstitch. Once you've sewed all four sides of the mushroom cap, flip the cap outside in.

STEP 3

Place different-sized spots in sporadic places around the cap and stitch into place with basic single stitches.

Teeny-Tiny Critters & Their Accessories

STEP 4

Pair the base of the mushroom to the mushroom cap, leaving just a slight margin of white showing at the outside of the cap. Stitch at the edge with a running stitch.

STEP 5

When you have just a small opening left, use toy stuffing to stuff the mushroom cap.

STEP 6

Once the mushroom is lightly filled, continue sewing the opening shut. From here, you can save the mushroom cap as a hat to sew onto your critters, or continue to make tiny mushrooms for your critters to frolic amongst.

STEP 7

Let's add the stem! Fold the stem piece in half and stitch the edges together along the side, leaving the ends open.

STEP 8

Open the stem to make a small tunnel shape. Match the base of the stem to one end of the tunnel shape and pin into place. Begin stitching around the diameter of the stem base.

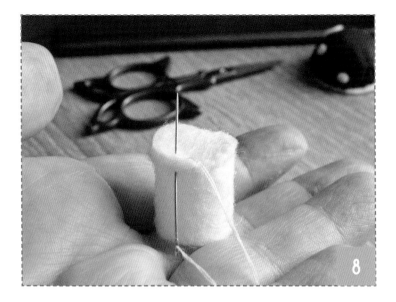

STEP 9

Gently fill the stem with toy stuffing. Pin the stem of the mushroom to the bottom base of the cap and stitch into place with a whipstitch.

Check out the next project for another
way to use the mushroom top—as a hat
for a cute little frog!

MUSHROOM FROG

For the ultimate cute and whimsical woodland creature, pair your miniature mushroom caps with one of your tiny felt frogs!

STEP 1

Begin by knotting your thread straight onto the middle base of the mushroom cap.

STEP 2

Send the needle through the middle top of the frog's back for just a small stitch.

STEP 3

Pull the thread tight, pulling the mushroom into place onto the frogs back. Hold the mushroom cap firmly in place while sending the needle through the cap base once again, and then back through the frog's back. Knot the thread under the mushroom and trim off the excess thread.

Teeny-Tiny Critters & Their Accessories

4

TINY DOLLS

& Dollhouses

DOLL

These dolls are the sweetest, tiniest little things. Keep a handful in your pocket for tiny companions on the go, as part of a miniature play set or dollhouse. These cuties are perfect for using up your felt and fabric scraps! Make them in an array of skin tones with tiny dresses of all colors.

STEP 1

Begin by cutting the doll's body and hair pattern from wool or wool blend felt.

Pattern on page 124

STEP 2

Using a small, tight running stitch, sew the hair to the body pieces. The back of the hair should be sewn just across the bottom of the head above the neck. Stitch the front hair piece just along the bangs and face.

STEP 3

Mark where you'd like to place the doll's eye with a fine-tipped marker or pencil. Create eyes with black embroidery thread or plastic doll eyes. Black seed beads would work very well too. Here I've used 2 mm black plastic doll eyes with posts and washers.

Tiny Dolls & Dollhouses

STEP 4

Create a nose in the middle of the face by making one straight stitch with embroidery thread of a contrasting color. Follow the same technique to make a mouth from a pink-hued embroidery thread. The stitch should be placed just below the nose and just a tad wider than the nose.

STEP 5

Cut a couple of pieces of chenille wire to sew into the doll's body. Hold the wire up to the doll to determine where to cut the pieces, and then gently bend the wire so that it will fit into the doll's limbs.

STEP 6

Match the front and back pieces of the doll. Tie off some thread to the inside of the doll's head just before the pigtail on the right. Begin stitching with a short, tight blanket or whipstitch. When you reach the pigtail, switch to a running stitch, and go back to the blanket or whipstitch just after the pigtail.

Switch thread colors when you reach the face and skin-tone-colored felt. Continue stitching along the edges of the felt, moving past the arm and leg.

STEP 7

Begin stuffing the dolls arm and legs with very small bits of stuffing at a time, pushing the stuffing into the limbs with the tool of your choice.

STEP 8

Once the limbs are fully stuffed, continue sewing past the second leg. When you reach the top of the leg, stop to stuff the limb.

STEP 9

Continue this way past the second arm, stopping once again to stuff the arm and the bottom parts of the body.

Tiny Dolls & Dollhouses

STEP 10

When you reach the doll's hair once again, switch thread colors and continue sewing until you've reach just past the second pig tail. Stuff the top of the body, neck, and head. Sew the last opening shut and tie off your thread.

STEP 11

I like to give the limbs a little bend. Gently turn up the arms and slightly bend the legs. It looks so cute!

DRESSES

Now move on to the dresses! I've created two patterns to choose from:
a super-cute fabric dress or a tiny felt dress. Both turn out adorably
but vary in difficulty to make.

The fabric dress can be a little tricky to sew because it is so tiny with very small
pieces. It requires longer sewing time and a hot iron to press down the edges.
But if you're willing to brave the task, it is well worth the effort!

The felt dress is fairly quick and easy. What I love most is that you can add your
own flair with some tiny embroidery! I'll show you how to add a tiny heart.

TINY FABRIC DRESS

STEP 1

Begin by cutting the fabric by tracing the pattern straight onto the fabric or taping the pattern to the fabric the same way you cut your felt.

Use a hot clothes iron to crease the edges of the fabric pieces as indicated on the pattern.

Pattern on page 124

STEP 2

Cut out a teeny-tiny pair of felt undergarments. Stitch the two pieces together at the sides and bottom. Flip the piece inside out to fit to the doll.

STEP 3

Stitch the edges of the fabric together with a small, closely stitched running stitch. Stitch along the outer and bottom edges of the skirt, sides and top of the dress bib, and straight down the middle of the dress straps.

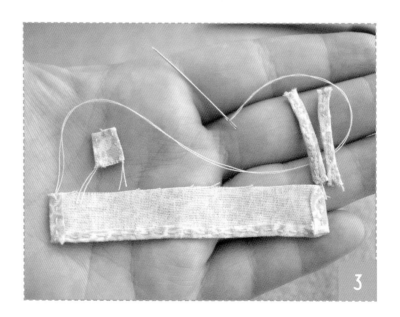

STEP 4

Place a wide, loose basting stitch along the top of the skirt. This will be used to pull the skirt into a bit of a ruffle. Pull the threads and skirt just long enough to fit around the doll and overlap a bit in the back.

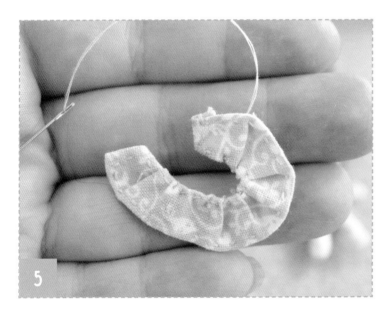

STEP 5

Fold the top over just a tad and iron into place. Stitch along the crease.

STEP 6

Find the middle of the skirt and sew the bib piece into place on the skirt. Next, sew the straps into place at the top of the bib.

STEP 7

Hold the dress up to the doll, folding the strap over to see where it will fall at the back of the dress. Stitch the strap to the inside back of the dress. Snip off any excess length of the strap, and repeat this step for the opposite dress strap. Fit the dress to the doll and overlap the skirt at the back. Stitch together the overlapping pieces at the back of the dress. Alternatively, you could sew in a miniature snap at the back for a removable dress.

Look at her sweet little pinafore.
Now she's ready to play!

TINY FELT DRESS

STEP 1

Begin by cutting the felt dress pattern so that you have two pieces: one for the front and one for the back.

Pattern on page 124

STEP 2

Stitch the side of the dress up on one side using a short, tight blanket or whipstitch. Start from the bottom and move your way upward.

STEP 3

Stitch together at the upper arm with just one or two stitches. Now you can add some embroidery to the dress! I've added a tiny and simple embroidered heart. The easiest way to create the heart is to split your embroidery thread down to two strands. Make a tiny "V" shape with just two stitches.

Tiny Dolls & Dollhouses

STEP 4

Fill in the "V" with another stitch or two, ending with a shorter stitch to make the heart shape.

STEP 5

Fit the dress to the doll and begin sewing the dress with the doll wearing it. Start at the shoulder, and then from the waist moving downward. Once you reach the bottom of the dress you can tie off your threads and you're done!

Using the techniques you've learned here,
you can make a wide variety of dolls wearing
different clothes, hairstyles, accessories, and more!

TEDDY BEAR

If you've been wanting to make the cutest teeny-tiny teddy bear ever, then you've come to the right place! These bears can be made in endless color combinations. Pair them with tiny felt overalls or either of the tiny doll dresses (pages 88-93).

STEP 1

Begin by cutting the tiny bear pattern from your choice of wool or wool-blend felt. Add some eyes with embroidery thread, seed beads, or 2mm plastic doll eyes.

Add a nose and mouth with embroidery. You can freehand embroider the nose and mouth or mark it in fine-tip pen first as a guide for your stitches. As always in tiny embroidery, make sure to split your embroidery thread down to one or two strands.

Pattern on page 124

STEP 2

Cut a couple of pieces of chenille wire to sew into the bear's body. Hold the wire up to the doll to determine where to cut the pieces, and then gently bend the wire so that it will fit into the bear's limbs.

STEP 3

Knot your thread to the inside of the bear's body. Match the front and back pattern pieces and begin stitching at the top of the head, just before the ear, using a short, tight blanket stitch or whipstitch. Sew along the edges going over the ear and down the face.

Tiny Dolls & Dollhouses

STEP 4

Continue stitching down one side of the bear's body, past the arm and to the inside of the leg while keeping the wire sandwiched between the layers of felt, so it's inserted into the bear's limbs.

STEP 5

Begin stuffing the bear's limbs by balling up tiny pieces of toy stuffing and gently stuffing them into the limbs with the tool of your choice. I like to use a toothpick or the end of an unwound paper clip.

STEP 6

Continue stitching past the opposite leg, stopping to stuff the leg. Then stitch past the arm and once again stop to stuff the arm and the body.

STEP 7

Once you reach the top of the neck, stop for a moment to stuff the rest of the body and the top of the neck. Continue sewing until you reach the top of the bear's head again, just past the ear.

STEP 8

Make sure to stuff each of the bear's ears before stuffing the head to the top. Stitch the last opening shut and tie off your thread.

STEP 9

Give the arms a little lift and the legs a bend.

STEP 10

Let's make some tiny overalls! Start by cutting the overalls from wool felt: one piece for the front and one for the back. Knot your thread to the inside of the felt and begin stitching down one side of the overalls with a short, tight blanket stitch or whipstitch. Tie off the thread when you reach the bottom of the leg.

STEP 11

Begin stitching again at the opposite side of the end of the leg, leaving the bottom open for the end of the bear's leg to fit through. Stitch together the inner edges of the legs of the overalls.

STEP 12

To finish the overalls, put them on the bear, pushing the bear's leg down into the already-sewn side. Knot your thread to the inside bottom of the opposite side of the overalls. Begin stitching up the leg, stitching the overalls straight onto the bear.

Tiny Dolls & Dollhouses

STEP 13

When you reach the top of the overalls, leave the thread dangling. You will use it to continue sewing the overall straps into place. Flip the bear over and tuck one side of the overall straps into the back of the pants. Send the needle through the side of the overalls and out of the strap to create a stitch to hold it in place.

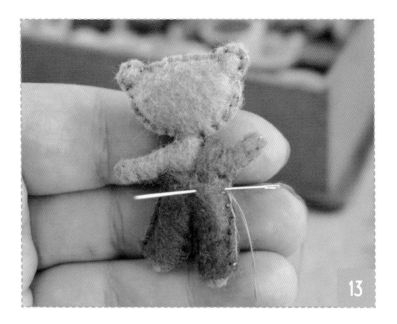

STEP 14

Tuck the second strap into the back of the pants. Send the needle once again through the back of the pants, then through the first strap and out of the second strap. You may want to add a stitch or two to each of the straps to further reinforce them.

Tie off the thread to the inside back
of the pants and you're done!

MUSHROOM DOLLHOUSE

Have you ever wished you could live in the forest in a tiny mushroom house? These mushroom houses are inspired by my childhood dreams of living in the forest like a tiny gnome.

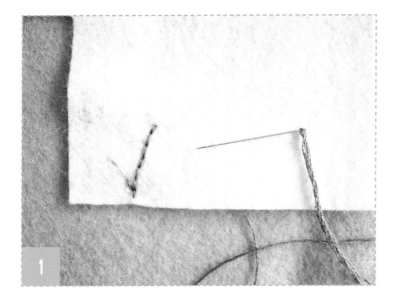

STEP 1

Begin by cutting the pattern pieces for the tiny mushroom house. I encourage you to get creative with your color choices. The walls of the house should be cut twice.

Start by adding some basic, beginner-friendly embroidery. Most of the embroidery consists of simple curved lines placed at different angles to make very basic flower stem shapes. These can be freehand stitched or sketched onto the felt with pencil or embroidery chalk.

Pattern on page 125

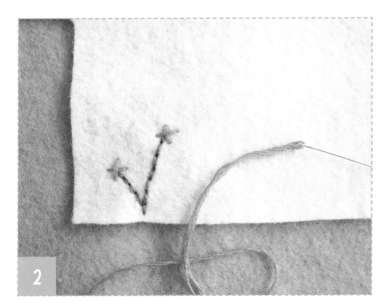

STEP 2

Begin with the flowers to the right of the door. Sketch two curved lines, one shorter and one longer, facing slightly away from each other.

Fill in the lines by embroidering a green stem on top of the sketched lines with a basic backstitch. At the top of the flower stems, place a small "X" with embroidery thread in the color of your choice.

STEP 3

Next, create a lazy daisy stitch around the "X" stitches. (See page 23 for a primer on making lazy daisy stitches.)

Tiny Dolls & Dollhouses

STEP 4

Next, add little mushrooms next to the flowers. Yes, we're putting mushrooms on a mushroom! These are different kinds of mushrooms. Start almost exactly as you did with the last set of flowers, sketching curved lines. For this set, make three curved lines all facing the same direction at different lengths.

STEP 5

Create the mushroom stems with a backstitch placed directly on top of the lines you just sketched. To create the mushroom caps, begin placing simple, horizontal straight stitches at the top of each stem.

Place stitches on top of stitches, making each one progressively shorter to the top of the mushroom. This will create a tiny mushroom-cap shape.

STEP 6

Now let's create some lovely flowers on the opposite side of the door. This time, make one long stem with several other stems branching from it.

STEP 7

Use a backstitch to fill in all of the flower stems and branching-off stems. To create a flower, begin making tiny French knots in clusters at the ends of each of the stems.

STEP 8

Add more mushrooms on the opposite side of the flowers. Get creative with colors or experiment with where you place the embroidered flowers and mushrooms.

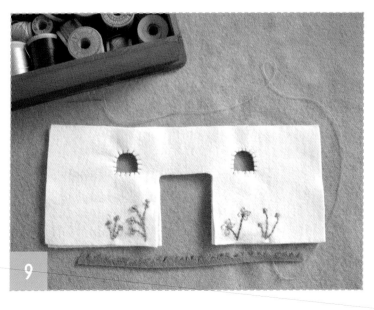

STEP 9

Pair the two pieces you cut for the walls of the house with the flowers facing to the front. Knot some thread off to the inside by one of the windows and begin stitching the outer edges of the windows with a short, tight blanket or whipstitch.

Tiny Dolls & Dollhouses

STEP 10

Stitch all the outer edges of the
mushroom house walls, excluding
one side.

STEP 11

 Fold the walls in on themselves and
overlap the back walls by ¼ inch (1/2
cm). Stitch the walls together along the
overlapped edges using a running stitch.

STEP 12

Switch to green thread and tie off your
thread to the inside bottom of the house
somewhere near the door. Match and pin
the grass pieces into place at the bottom
of the house. Stitch the grass into place
along the bottom edge of the house using
a running stitch.

STEP 13

Pair two of the circular pieces for the mushroom house floor and stitch them together at the outer edges using a short, tight blanket or whipstitch. Pin the mushroom house walls to the floor. There will be a space between the walls and the outer diameter of the floor.

STEP 14

Next, begin creating the mushroom cap for the top of the house. Start by stitching together the edges of the top of the mushroom. Knot your thread off to the underside of the mushroom near the top. Sew these edges together from top to bottom, working your way around all four sides of the mushroom. Flip the mushroom cap inside out.

STEP 15

Sew spots of different sizes scattered randomly around the mushroom.

STEP 16

Match the top of the mushroom to the circular bottom mushroom piece. There will be about ⅛ inch (3 mm) of space around the outer edge of the mushroom.

Then gently stuff the mushroom with toy stuffing, and sew the opening shut.

STEP 17

Match the door pieces and stitch around the window and outer edges with a short, tight blanket or whipstitch.

STEP 18

Attach the door to one side by placing stitches to work as "hinges" in an "X" formation at the edge of the door. Add a snap to the opposite side to hold the door shut.

To finish, pin the mushroom cap
to the top of the walls and stitch in place
with a whipstitch.

TREE STUMP HOUSE

One of my favorite things to do is walk in the woods and forage for treasures. I often pick up birch bark during my travels. I just love the simple and rustic beauty of a birch tree! I've created this tiny dollhouse inspired by a birch tree, with a cute acorn on top.

Pattern on pages 126–127

STEP 1

Begin by cutting the pattern pieces for the tree-stump house. Because this project is designed to look like a birch tree, a white or an off-white colored felt works best. Choose earthy colors for the base and woody beige and brown colors for the acorn top and door. The walls of the house should be cut twice.

To start, split the embroidery thread into three strands for the first layer of embroidery. Add some basic embroidery to the top piece. Most of the embroidery consists of simple curved and straight lines to mimic the pattern on a birch tree, which looks a bit like eyes. Scatter some "eye" shapes all over the outer walls. Then go back and add scattered horizontal and straight lines. You can freehand embroider or sketch onto the felt with pencil or embroidery chalk.

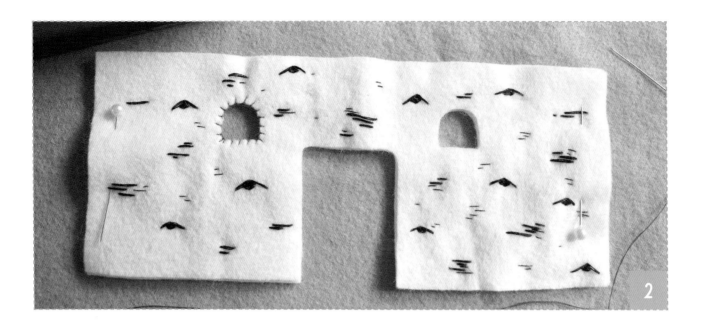

STEP 2

Once you've embroidered across the pattern piece, tie off your thread to the inside. Now go back in and add a little finer detailing. Split the thread down to only one strand and add some more horizontal lines and dashes here and there across the surface.

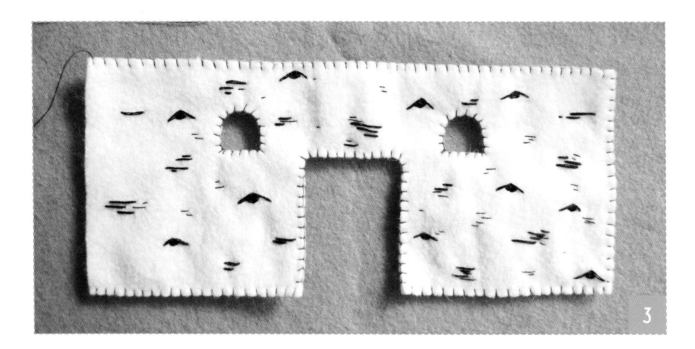

STEP 3

Pair together and pin the two wall-pattern pieces. Then begin stitching them together at the windows. Tie off your thread to the inside near one of the windows. Stitch around the outer edges of the windows using a short, tight blanket or whipstitch.

Now move on to stitching the walls together at the outer borders. Begin by tying off your thread to the inside at the bottom-left corner. Stitch along the border on three sides: the bottom, right, and top. Leave the left edge open and raw.

STEP 4

Fold the walls in on themselves and overlap the backs by about ¼ inch (1/2 cm). Stitch the walls together along the overlapped edges with a running stitch.

STEP 5

Move on to stitching the base of the house into place and adding some embroidery. You should have two base pieces.

Start by stitching the top of the house to one piece of the base. To do this, pin the house onto the base, somewhat centering the birch-tree walls. Tie off your thread to the bottom of the base piece near the doorway of the house. Use a whipstitch to hold the house on the base. Stitch all the way around the base of the walls, tying off your thread when you reach the opposite side of the doorway.

STEP 6

Using all six strands of a piece of embroidery thread, scatter French knots all over to look like flowers and moss. Choose three to four colors, including one or two for flowers. The rest should be green for moss.

Using one color at a time, scatter the French knots all around the outer edges. Once you've added embroidery all the way around the edges (leaving room for more colors, of course!), switch colors and add some more. Continue until you've decorated the whole base.

Tiny Dolls & Dollhouses

STEP 7

Pair the second piece of the base with the bottom of the house. Stitch them into place around the outer edges with a blanket or whipstitch.

STEP 8

Match up the door pieces and stitch around the window and outer edges with a short, tight blanket or whipstitch. Then attach the door to one side by placing stitches to work as "hinges" in an "X" formation at the edge of the door. Add a snap to the opposite side to hold the door shut.

STEP 9

Next, create the acorn cap for the top of the house. Start by stitching together the gusset edges of the top of the acorn cap. Sew these edges together from top to bottom, working your way around all four sides of the pattern piece. Flip the acorn cap inside out.

STEP 10

To add detail to the acorn cap, place some embroidered "X" shapes throughout the cap.

STEP 11

Let's create a cute leaf-and-stem detail for the top of the house! Start by adding some detail to the leaf via embroidered ridges along the leaf. I've used a double strand of embroidery thread and added the details with a backstitch.

STEP 12

Roll one side of the stem inward and stitch it into place with a basic running stitch.

STEP 13

Roll the opposite side of the stem over the already rolled and stitched side of the stem. Secure it with a whipstitch at the back of the leaf.

STEP 14

Knot some thread at the top middle of the acorn cap. Send the needle and thread through the bottom of the leaf and out of the top of the stem. Push the leaf down onto the cap so that it sits in place on top of the acorn cap.

Send the needle back down through the stem and into the cap once again. Switch to a whipstitch to sew the stem in place at the base of the stem and the top of the cap.

Push the acorn cap onto the top of the walls and stitch it in place with a whipstitch just at the gusset seams with a single stitch or two.

Tie off your thread, hiding it under
the cap, to finish the project!

5

PATTERNS

FOX

See project directions on page 26.

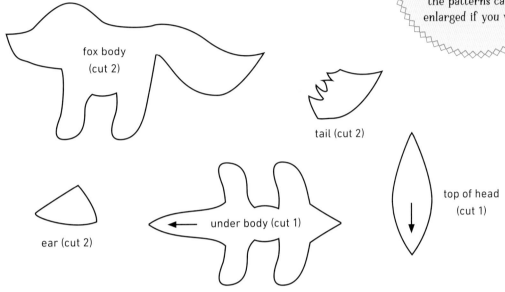

fox body
(cut 2)

tail (cut 2)

top of head
(cut 1)

ear (cut 2)

under body (cut 1)

CAT

See project directions on page 34.

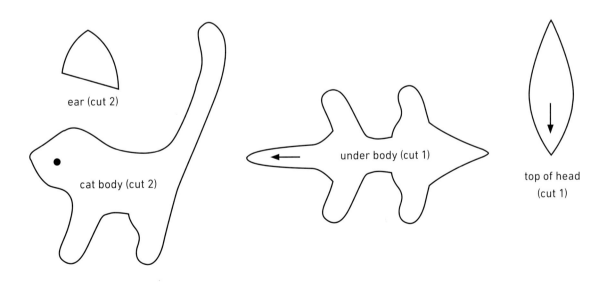

ear (cut 2)

cat body (cut 2)

under body (cut 1)

top of head
(cut 1)

Patterns

DOG

See project directions on page 42.

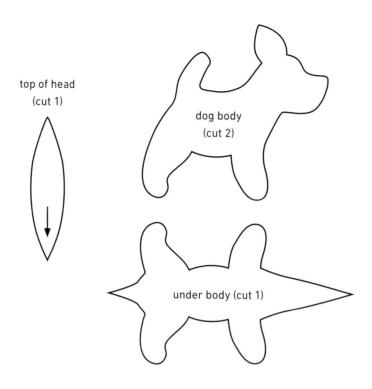

top of head
(cut 1)

dog body
(cut 2)

under body (cut 1)

PET BED

See project directions on page 54.

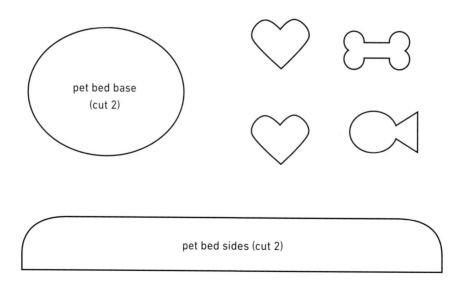

pet bed base
(cut 2)

pet bed sides (cut 2)

DOGHOUSE

See project directions on page 48.

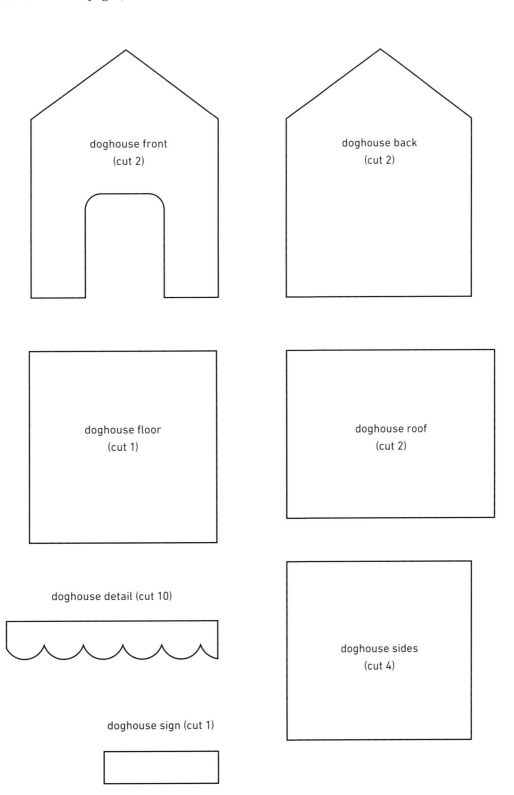

doghouse front
(cut 2)

doghouse back
(cut 2)

doghouse floor
(cut 1)

doghouse roof
(cut 2)

doghouse detail (cut 10)

doghouse sides
(cut 4)

doghouse sign (cut 1)

SKUNK

See project directions on page 58.

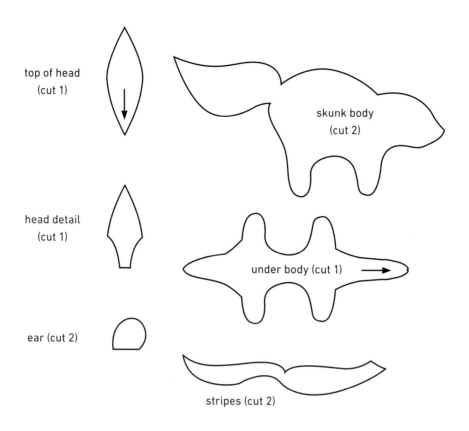

top of head
(cut 1)

skunk body
(cut 2)

head detail
(cut 1)

under body (cut 1)

ear (cut 2)

stripes (cut 2)

FROG

See project directions on page 66.

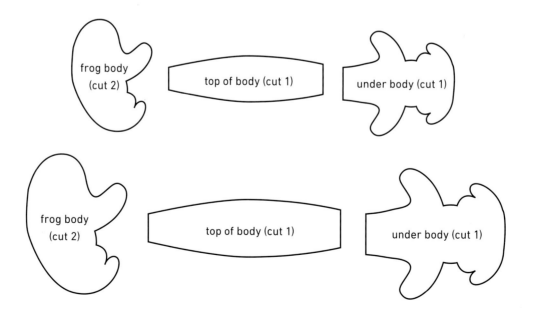

frog body
(cut 2)

top of body (cut 1)

under body (cut 1)

frog body
(cut 2)

top of body (cut 1)

under body (cut 1)

MUSHROOM

See project directions on page 72

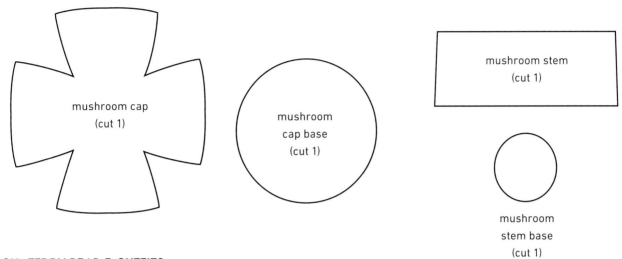

mushroom cap
(cut 1)

mushroom
cap base
(cut 1)

mushroom stem
(cut 1)

mushroom
stem base
(cut 1)

DOLL. TEDDY BEAR & OUTFITS

See project directions on pages 88 and 91.

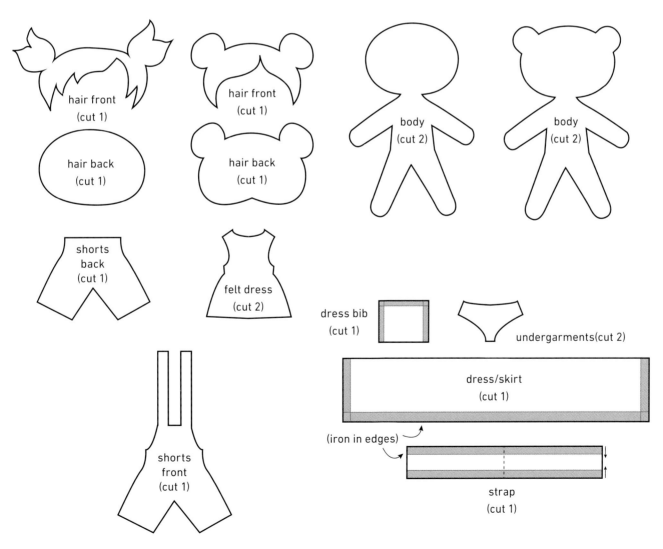

hair front
(cut 1)

hair back
(cut 1)

hair front
(cut 1)

hair back
(cut 1)

body
(cut 2)

body
(cut 2)

shorts
back
(cut 1)

felt dress
(cut 2)

dress bib
(cut 1)

undergarments (cut 2)

dress/skirt
(cut 1)

(iron in edges)

strap
(cut 1)

shorts
front
(cut 1)

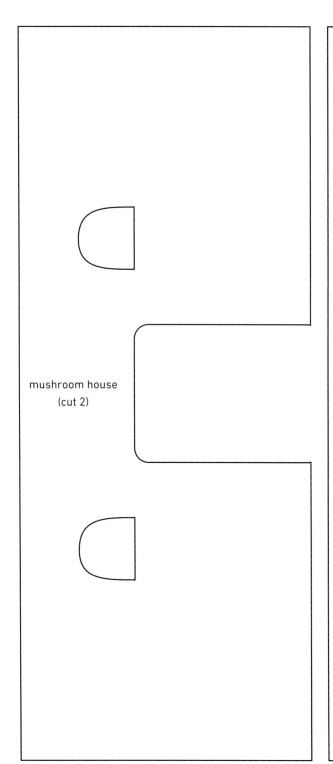

mushroom house
(cut 2)

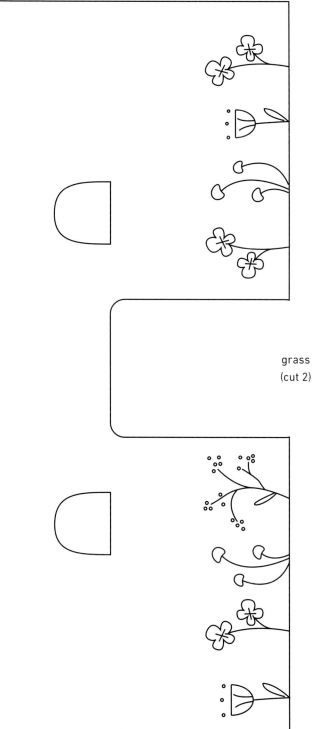

grass
(cut 2)

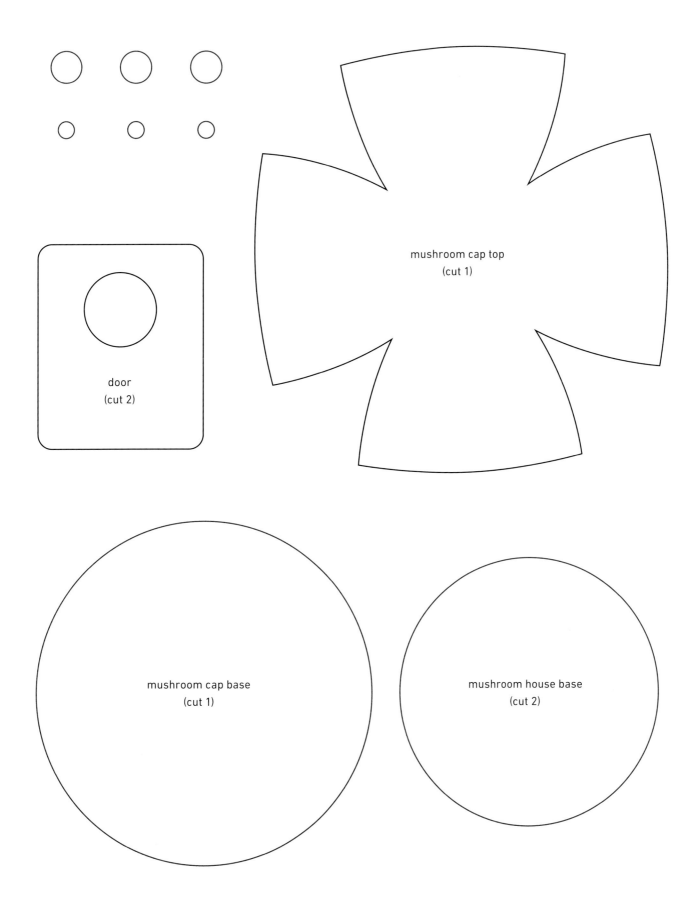

door
(cut 2)

mushroom cap top
(cut 1)

mushroom cap base
(cut 1)

mushroom house base
(cut 2)

TREE STUMP HOUSE

See project directions on page 110.

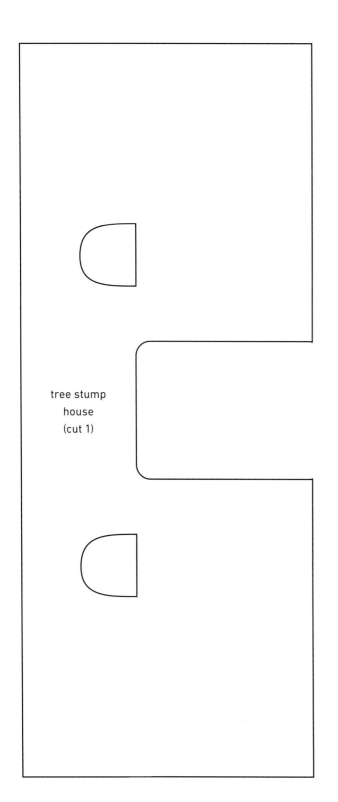

tree stump
house
(cut 1)

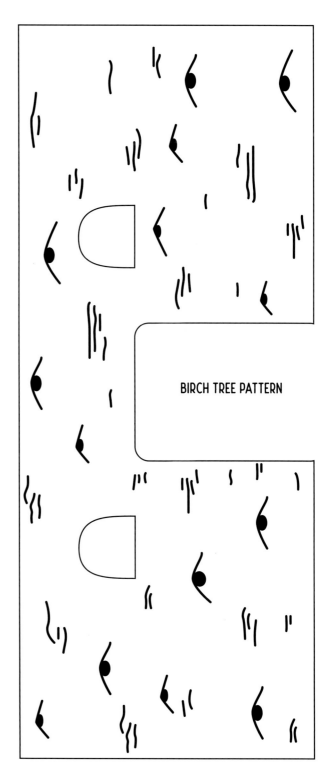

BIRCH TREE PATTERN

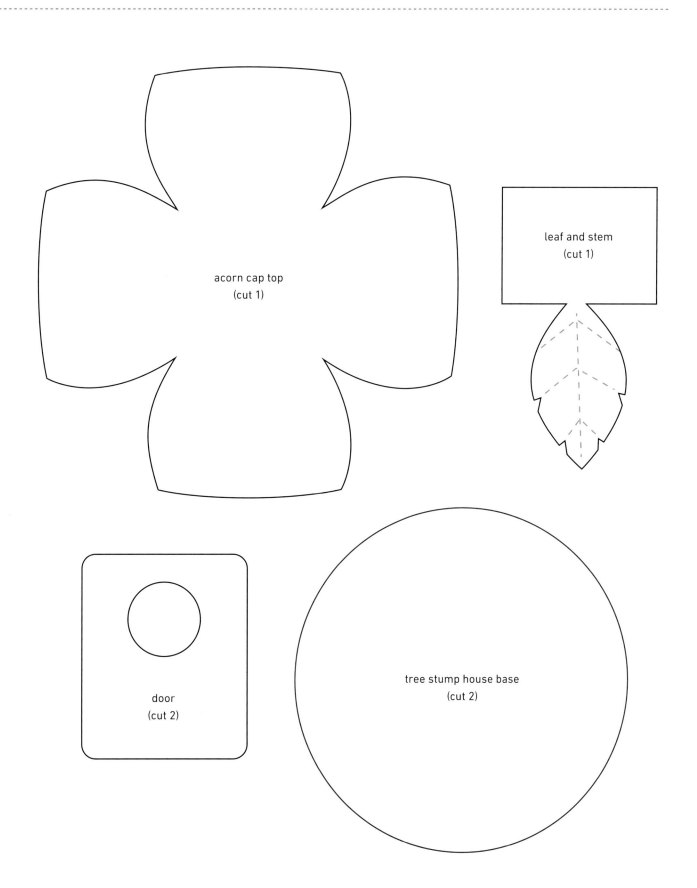

acorn cap top
(cut 1)

leaf and stem
(cut 1)

door
(cut 2)

tree stump house base
(cut 2)

ABOUT THE AUTHOR

Delilah Iris is a felt artist, maker, and graphic designer. She launched her small business, DelilahIris Designs, an online shop featuring a brand of hand-sewn felt toys and dolls, in the fall of 2013. Delilah's creations have been covered by news features in her home state of Maine multiple times, as well as in international magazines, such as *Taproot* Magazine and *Homespun* Magazine.

Delilah's passions lie in sharing art and creativity, as well as passing on creative ideas and skills. "I thrive in creativity and am driven by sharing the creative process with others," she says.

Delilah creates easy-to-follow sewing patterns that are simple to make for the average beginner. "Hand sewing is such a timeless craft with so many uses! I find I love to work in fiber and hand sewing the most of all artistic mediums. My patterns and kits are a fantastic way to learn to sew while creating something wonderful! You'll surprise yourself with what you can make."

Delilah grew up south of Boston in Massachusetts but currently resides in rural Maine, in the heart of Skowhegan, a quaint and artsy community located along the Kennebec River. She draws inspiration from the lush forests and meadows of Maine, its wildlife, and her children, who received the first felt toys she ever created.